D0558347

JUMPING
THE
LINE

≈

TED
GREENWALD

ROOF BOOKS
NEW YORK

ISBN 0-937804-77-0
Library of Congress Card Catolog No. 99-070144

Cover photo & design © Les Levine 1998
Back cover photo © Lloyd McNeill 1998

Roof Books are distributed by Small Press Distribution,
1341 Seventh Avenue, Berkeley, CA. 94710-1403.
800-869-7553

State of the Arts

This book was made possible, in part, by a grant from the
NYSCA New York State Council on the Arts.

Roof Books are published by
Segue Foundation
303 East 8th Street
New York, New York 10009

To JTMC, with love

JUMPING
THE
LINE

Brush with death
Not a pretty picture
But a series of pictures

Each hole-like stroke
Secreting enemies
Absorbed in conversation

It's incredible
This unbelievableness
It's no nonsense

This sensible shoe
But what were you thinking
When you thought

But what were you thinking
When you thought
This is happening to me

This is happening to me
A must-see summer
Film chemistry sitcom uh-huh

Film chemistry sitcom uh-huh
A must-see summer
You could build a porch around

Listen for the slightest move
According to bible voices
Tuned to the food

Hmm, this is delicious
And so are you
It's big as life

This is outdoors itself
Emphasis on relationship
Putter with frame

Hormones kick in
The door to your floor
Sealing fate

Millions moviegoers missing
Just brown and serve
Makes a scenic loop

But above all
Below-average waiting
Watches only edges

Don't might be there
Be there
Train's last car

Be there
Train's last car
Talks to your food

Talks to your food
But never listens
Put out the lights

Put out the lights
But never listens
Thin bulb captions

Leaders and followers cut
Cut to the chaise
Wend way to

But never better than
You only thing you breathe
Arguing what thighs

As ashtrays fill with lies
Dew powdery liftoff
Will be no bakeoff

Frog says Croak
A willingness to please pass
This way and that

By dreams
I mean for dreams
Di di duh

Carry over into
Talking reunion blew who
Bird says Tweet

And so you shall
So shall we all shall
Take a moment out

So shall we all shall
Take a moment out
Just think

Just think
Abbreviate total splendor
Spent big time

Spent big time
Abbreviate total splendor
In a wink

Try on pronoun for size
Run into coincidentally
Not the usual

The usual belongs
How would you say it
In your own Language

Leaping at pure change
Develop into luggage
And so we shall

To point at which
Bump into
Know you somewhere

Resist buying
And was gone
Quick Hide

Apparently silver
Jangle notes rise
Frozen on windows

Nature reruns
Stop for a bite
Build bridge to

Stop for a bite
Build bridge to
Bar after bar

Bar after bar
Keep watching green
Not really thirsty

Not really thirsty
Keep watching green
Weed out weeds

Bench press neon
Blinking dumbell curls
Tweets forewarned

Need to ask
Need to know
Elephant compartment

As you move
Imagine how far
Make you star

Out there in the jungle
It's your own hair
And will continue to grow

Glow for the rest your life
If you're a youngster
Reading at home

Horseshit to rush hour nod
So great to come
Home to no one

Strong dream whiff
Hard work Hard times
Hand does hair things

Hard work Hard times
Hand does hair things
With all due respect

With all due respect
Wanna blowjob
Get fucked

Get fucked
Wanna blowjob
Going to fuck you up

Got a plan
Going down in flames in
Conceivable but unusual

Please take your change
Filter through roadie armies
Open to question

Topless documents
Peopleless estuaries
Dap miniscule vivid pinions

Can you describe
How you feel
Exactly Exactly

Listen for the break
Get goofy with
Blend freeze frames

Duck under awning
Call out to
Blender mush

Only some talk
Beats having to
Think about

Beats having to
Think about
Underwater moan

Underwater moan
Love me phone
Write home about

Write home about
Love me phone
Forget about past

Crossing out
Is
Crossing over

Forget you came with
Original packaging
Down to small screws

Add up to
One piece fits all
Nail to nail

14

Egg drop soup
Prime ordinance
Follow instructions

That socialize
With no one wise
Feel free to leave

This corpse-like tree
Tomorrow is another
How you say

Pay up
D side B side
Hear the eggs drop

D side B side
Hear the eggs drop
Personal flotation

Personal flotation
D vice for D vising
Shade eyes

Shade eyes
D vice for D vising
Midnight J walk

Pear blip
Last forever
Seems like

Hand to D liver
Which brings us to
Swamped mop

Jot down same
Before swallowing
Rev N genes

Can you describe
The magic moment
Without falling

Through the floor
In quotes
The often referred to

Just before
Don't remember
When Or what

Or then some
SRO matter
Fried Too stressed

SRO matter
Fried Too stressed
Need to egg on

Need to egg on
Keep hand in
Serene off season

Serene off season
Keep hand in
The

Freezing point
Lost-in-thought D
Meaning of life

Showcase saying
Entrees run around
Zip down to

Dish a tire swing
Fleshout underline
Hilit slurps

Quack quack
It's for you
Stranger central

Info fronds
Cool drinks to
Name emblazon on

Company to
Longitude am gone
Don't wait up

Play for fool
All smiles
Got carry away

All smiles
Got carry away
Daybreak

Daybreak
In the conversation
Smiles away

Smiles away
In the conversation
Who refer to

Strange way showing
Rope down
Window of

Waders
Under words
More wordy

Cloud hovers
Eye follow
Mind off

Sometimes
It's not such
A good idea

To speak your mind
Don't mind
If I do

If I don't
See you when
You get back

So what
I been
Jerking off

I been
Jerking off
To you

To you
For umpteen
Years

Years
For umpteen
Meaningful smile

Bivalves
In your court
Ineffable

Without F
Or table turns
All the way

Around a turn
Phrase heard
Please pass

Watch
Get up
Wander window

Look out
Sparrow quarrel
For what

Day ahead
Same sequence
About

Day before
Wash face
Sit down to

Wash face
Sit down to
Cigaret

Cigaret
Sip coffee Smoke
Exit right

Exit right
Sip coffee Smoke
Notice move

Light up
Buildings
Things

To do To don't
Shower
Towel dry

Shave
Dress
Off

Escape from
Some version
Of surf

Put on
Gravity remove
From

Yon to hither
Inescapable
Raw snow

Hat
But first
I tell you

But first
I tell you
You can tell

You can tell
And secondly
All we

All we
And secondly
No place

For the curtain
To come down
Window still

Open
Never is
Leave

Make be
Refer above
Word sonar

Head filling news
Actual are
Trickle down party

Livewire old
Watch out for
We lie against

Toe plays
Kneejerk response
If not for

Moreover
Nothing for you
Means nothing

Nothing for you
Means nothing
Alligator clip

Alligator clip
Blank out
One for all

One for all
Blank out
The one you're with

Sudden soak
Too-ish drama
Windbag

Play over
Worn flat
Move longing

Xed chemistry
Runway lights
Beddy-bye

Talk Listen
When do you ever
I don't see your face

You don't get paid
No matter
Oh, baby, oh

Know nothing
Right or wrong
Lobster bib

Let us
Hold harmless
These claws

Hold harmless
These claws
In a phrase

In a phrase
Waive your right
Hand

Hand
Waive your right
To hand

It to you
Without once
Weren't listening

Taking away
From what
Were you thinking

Sometimes tops
Sometimes bottomless
Pit Spit out

Need to be needed
Imagine dough
Fold yourself neat

Open shudder
Seems to warn
Twinight doubleheader

Around corner
Square with
Body outline

Envelope plan
Years in tenses
Why bother

Years in tenses
Why bother
Brand name

Brand name
Hand-held
Documented

Documented
Hand-held
Flurry of activity

Seems strange
Pretty daze
Ambling whoops

Mix air brakes
Solo bakeoff
What have you

Fat and salt
Small medium
At large

Flyer
Looks interesting
Check out

Nobody has yet said
Be grateful Get ahead
Wonder why

Mustard read my mind
Bump Goose
Working here

Is what it's like
Being dead
Won't stick

Being dead
Won't stick
Lo tack woe

Lo tack woe
Misery's hoof
Lands wherever

Lands wherever
Misery's hoof
Mystery guest cosign

Who's on whose
But I wonder
Can you believe

Maybe you meet
Someone great
Is the answer

Alarm warns
Walk on by
After the fact

Get the fuck
Out of here
Society's to blame

Reality: You
Win some You lose
Some Not cute

The computer
Figures it out
Put it in

Yeah Put it in
Software lowdown
Compares up floors

Software lowdown
Compares up floors
Mistook for

Mistook for
Long lost love
Rewax

Rewax
Long lost love
So it goes

The door opens
Forget the others
Mind matters

Large object
Send fax
Belong home

Ground up pop
Innocent bystanders
Stand around

Haircut does wonders
Step up Take swing
Remember which door

When we last heard
Our friends face tundra
Ironic good-for-you heros

Line snakes
Down mirage before
Afternoon   Main Street

Likes like A Listener
Air moves me over
Cool inside (see dive)

Air moves me over
Cool inside (see dive)
Water me, please

Water me, please
Forget to break
Blow lights

Blow lights
Forget to break
The other side of town

No underwear (see gown)
Breezy, less humid
Maybe fake storm

Real storm yellow light
Refreeze green
Trim top with sides

Shadowy entrance
Standup yonder
Loosen screwhead

Gaunt stems
Wallet-size entanglements
Do-over dew

Lay down the lawn
Play dead
Without a moon

Circle around
Lose everything
Once in awhile

At once
One thing only
That's what

One thing only
That's what
How do

How do
End of time
Work back

Work back
End of time
As if

Say you will
Won't hear me
Complain Complain

Flowery surface
One size fits all
Pops lure

View with bite
Tooth remarks
Splendid turnovers

Don't worry
Your little head,
Tiny person

Of the personal
Persuasion, we shall
Embark on instruments

Lulling the sirens
So we can enter
Filling the shoes

Kindness milky
You shoulda been there
Nothing to get

You shoulda been there
Nothing to get
Hang up

Hang up
I'm on the phone
Present company except

Present company except
I'm on the phone
Filling out a form

Where name goes
There goes I
Unable to light

Keep moving keep
Moving, almost morning
Sometime soon

Palms up and out
Don't stop now
Us more fool

Dream pull
So damn hard
Take back

To a simple time
Drool runs
In the streets

Dream place where
You happen
To be

The only and one
Sort of
Crawl back

Sort of
Crawl back
Portrait becomes

Portrait becomes
Landscape
Over and under

Over and under
Landscape
Believe my luck

If go real fast
Nothing reminds
Of anything

You can write
Home in on
Home about

But weather
Another luxury
Phrases accordingly

The first line
In a long line
All jaw

Twice at once
All job
Align

But thighs
Hands, say
Talk digitally

Numbered amongst
Cool drink
Looks rain

Cool drink
Looks rain
Too many maybes

Too many maybes
Bring down
Spirit level

Spirit level
Bring down
Topspin eyeline

Longing
Burst bubble
No trouble

Linger over
Not again
Light flickers

Legs around
Measured in feet
Inches longing

Fun never sets
Over Rover
Calendar moves

In on trends
No bone dogs
Bow totally

Wowed (erase)
Born riding
Each era sure

Shoes step out
Debone delight
Easy chew

Debone delight
Easy chew
When ask you

When ask you
You all right
Out light

Out light
You all right
Can rub off

Long way round
Come here
On the phone

Bio tick tock
Pure purr
Therapy therapy

Nifty, but
Gentle breeze
And cow

What's-more stench
Appeal that onion
Come in Sent down

Ahead of time
Won't come in
Dunking always

Guess nothing new
Air moves
Air guitar

Word for earn
Speculation breeds
More bidders

Speculation breeds
More bidders
Surprise jump

Surprise jump
Chameleon vocals
Catch train

Catch train
Chameleon vocals
Stand moot

Sure great
Not the point
Daybuilt movie

Give me bunny
Told different
Pick seams

Give me bunny
Pick seams
Apart from what

Pick up on
Fan-like bottom
Line to center

And you know
Just know
Who you are

No getting away
This summer
About it

Something like
Pause
Get up Pee

Pause
Get up Pee
Dress down

Dress down
To where
You understand

You understand
To where
Raining out

Have some heart
To say
In passing

You really
Think that
Watch the hole

Recognize from
Somewhere deep
Heart ripped

Get up
Do your shit
Go home

But you're home
Already
That was quick

Never left
The house
But

You righted
Scribbling
Ample picture

Scribbling
Ample picture
Mind

Mind
If I do
So what

So what
If I do
Complete thought

Tonite's the
Without the "Gee!"
The nite

It says
There on
Forthwith

The marquee
Hanging
Every word

Sit for hours
Watch the door
For

Death warmed
Over walks in
For

The umpteenth time
Coughdrop dessert
For

Only you
Road ties
Heavens lead to

Road ties
Heavens lead to
Leanto

Leanto
Music shelters
Mag view

Mag view
Music shelters
For

Only you
Breathe into
The pronouns

Only you
For nouns
For verbs

Air removes
Thank you
Call again

Kill the shoes
Where we came in
Depends on

Hanging around
For something
On your every word

To happen
Flyer miles
Any point to

Flyer miles
A period
In what

A period
In what
You're doing

You're doing
No thing
Makes sense

Makes sense
No thing
The object of

Your every word
Mind twins
Double back on

Motorama moods
Flags flutter over
Shack opens

Coffee can't Won't
Do you wanna
Fuck it!

Saving the best
Part for elastic
We're not there

At least, not yet
Willing to admit
Maybe edgy

Adjectives (blub)
Not good thing
Forget native speaker

Monorail funnel
Which brings me
To the part

Which brings me
To the part
In the telling

In the telling
This is the phone
Please pick up

Please pick up
This is the phone
Relive moment

Hand reaches
Around from behind
Extreme adjective

Lacey remember when
Deucey bruise
Eye craze

Priority delivery
Almost important
Pigheaded

Good time having
No band No hands
Maybe shoulda got it

End up tragic
Too melodramatic
Where's the EXIT

But never know
Stand up now, to
Midnight coming through

Thick and thin
Dough rises
Air pocket

Dough rises
Air pocket
Rip your locket

Rip your locket
Out of those barrettes
Melt down

Melt down
Out of those barrettes
Noteshape hairs

Curl nerve ends
Energy befriends
Hang from food chain

Beyond talk
Way past chalk
Celery stalks tonight

Beyond yonder
Applause delete
Direct each feet

Bills chase bills
Silent carpet
Treatment lookover

Chuckle Buckle up
Bottle spitting image
More one good time

Believe me you
Who's confused
Around much any more

Come to pass
Way going
Bored to

Way going
Bored to
96 tears

96 tears
You're saying it
Strange dream

Strange dream
You're saying it
And wonderful

Meaning what
Would stop you
Howl at moon

Body up
Tiptoe blasé
Brain stem wind

Through there
Our own pictures
Sell the album

Looks like rain
Walk the dog
Forget the money

Don't forget me
I forgot you
When was that?

Something comes back
Wait and see
Tonguetip Yup

Daily, more often
Span the narrows
Out to lunch

Span the narrows
Out to lunch
Block out

Block out
Worth bottling
At sea

At sea
Worth bottling
Week after next

Pencil-in place
Time to
Put out the cat

Lonesome windows
Freakout .
Prevent leaks

Won't ever stop
Road ends
Where to now

Up in the night
Mood tinkering
Shapeless wandering

Under each thought
Carry to
A logical conclusion

Include sandwiches
This particular winter
Too foregone

Need a rest
Drift off to sleep
Choose dream

Drift off to sleep
Choose dream
Pieces

Pieces
Total recall
Cold water

Cold water
Total recall
Can't stand

To sit
This one out
Of here

Only seems like
An eternity
Rain

Down upon
Your passages
Eyes wide

Garden largeness
Would wax
Helicopter liftoff

Hanging out
Pass the road potatoes
Could May

R likely
To
Wear thin

Take place
Give it to M
Who's there

Give it to M
Who's there
Who cares

Who cares
Right now
Forget who

Forget who
Right now
Neats you

Place under
Describe Hardly
Petal depression

So (you) say
This way
Me go

Go sleep
Go team
On the go

But it's home
Look too great
Flattery's vanity

Enough about me
Enough me
To last last laugh

New development
Due date
He did observe

Come down
Come dawn
Who could forget

Come dawn
Who could forget
Money

Money
On oozy
Recommendation

Recommendation
On oozy
Mediocre pulse

Lightbulbs meet
The pages
Turn

The feeling
On you
Through

Their letters
Seeking bettering
Coulda did

Slid aside
Grab something
To eat

Something
To say you're sorry
But what now

What if
Familiar face
Snap

Call collect
Collect on it
Come in

Collect on it
Come it
Do your shit

Do your shit
Go home
Long away

Long away
Go home
Continuous show,

No waiting
Move to the rear
Plenty room inside

Get lost in
With a story
You're in it

Without hat
Coatless
Safe passage

Stay fresh
Stay pressed
Keep it up

Mouth dry
Wet lip
Looking down

Think up
Stay in touch
Float free

When you call
Think of me
You will

Think of me
You will
Go see

Go see
What you think
Answer ring

Answer ring
What you think
Touch stays

Born days
Dead doze off
B-b-b

Banana
Bandstand
Better half

Same smile
Stay face
Keep off grass

Enjoy the show
Past caring
Often enough

To be inspiring
Inquiring after you
Oblique light

Moving on
When
Time's not right

Goodbye
Is
Not goodnight

Is
Not goodnight
Don't sit

Don't sit
Nothing happening
Around

Around
Nothing happening
From scratch

Built to
Going fast
Dry eye

Looking over
Misshear flatout
Just about

I'm doing here
What am I
Doing Here

Force of nature
Nothing about
Nothing else

And did do
Forget well-liked
Be true

Which is only right
Fuck friends
They disappear

Around bends
Their own design
Wear out

Their own design
Wear out
Take clue

Take clue
About how close
Bridge moan

Bridge moan
About how close
History tucks in

By being there
When you least
Of all

Expect nothing less
Complete attention
Getting device

Other side
Needs equal time
Roll over

But then I woke
Above and beyond
Mere beauty

Is your beauty parlor
Lit from within
By words

Dripping from your roof
Take in the view
Breaking platelets

Across your center stage
Bird groups
Walk in your door

Bird groups
Walk in your door
Botany mechanics

Botany mechanics
Open your windows
Wider still

Wider still
Open your windows
Whole dazzle

Front delight
Cover to cover
Read your biography

Traffic covers
Legs and arms
Fuse to take your side

Just look
Just think
Just *think*

Just between foods
So deep
You turn over

Sleep 2 hours
More than
Your usual

Time to
Hit the dreams
Whoever shows

Enjoy
Their mere presence
How like you

Their mere presence
How like you
Say something

Say something
To summarize
Eye color

Eye color
To summarize
Hang out

Afternoon imagined
Blazetinged worry
Will they

Question marks
Dangle wind chimes
Along the ears

Exclaiming points
Our precursors
Follow deeper

Don't stop now
Who'd want to
Get off the body

Don't look now
Who thinks they
Know what you

Look like Look
Like one of those
Total sex giants

Ignite the sheet
Woven from gauze
Hint variety juices

Woven from gauze
Hint variety juices
Point A

Point A
Being the following
Hmm, hello

Hmm, hello
Being the following
Don't think anything

Get away with
Like minded redemption
Coupon for eternity

Make room for
Wonderful cries luggage
All-hole waterfalls

To write home
About lightning
Genes show through

Lose your place
In line
Skate too close

Get over
In your arms
No other moment

Combine to take
A breath
No matter who

Heart up
And grab at
What did you expect

And grab at
What did you expect
Run motor

Run motor
Off cross
At the mouth

At the mouth
Off cross
Laden with spoons

Dip into also-ran
Take breath away
To almost say

How you spend
How you spend
Your money

Your business
Defy gravity
June moon

Where you want
To play you lay
Your head down

Dump software
Under drawers
For a rainy day

Enough body
For each brain
To wile away

Your ailing saw
See over
Your ghost

See over
Your ghost
Speaks well of you

Speaks well of you
Without reservation
Rows and columbine

Rows and columbine
Without reservation
You're making something

You're making
A fucken hot rod
Tuned right

Stop signs purr
Edge of town
Check gauges

Hum to
The accelerator
On ramp

Drab with-itness
Who it
Considers what

The best such
La la
Strum arguments

Hard borne string
Pearls for lips
Entirely gather

The last last meal
Your average
Nostalgia vacuum cleaner

Your average
Nostalgia vacuum cleaner
Bends toward

Bends toward
Radio towers over
Rivulets pool

Rivulets pool
Radio towers over
Gumball warble

Hand cups
Ear bent
Toward forward

Less we forget
Pattern oven
Butter red

In no uncertain
Worm turns
Our guarantee

All clear
Take the lead
Stand up, already

Sit down, already
Get lost
Enough is never

Enough is inside
Out of sugar
Bring back cremora

And your panorama
Dusting the gloom
Raking your gravel

Dusting the gloom
Raking your gravel
Outside looking in

Outside looking in
Worry worry
No care how do

No care how do
Worry worry
Butt out

How lovely too
How do
You unscrew

Is morning glory
Evening the score
By gum

Get out your thumb
Look backward
Yum!

Pompoms
Cutting edge technology
Take off your games of chance

Head swimming
Forget which shore
Anxious sizzling

Streamers
Between each cloud
Dress to access

Closing ceremony
Deliver us from swivels
What good it does

Deliver us from swivels
What good it does
But owns up

But owns up
Pure lure
Fixings

Fixings
Pure lure
Splice quote on limb

Who thought
We talk
We meet like this

Invisible line
In common with
Real good time

Letter perfect missive
Wash ashore
Whichever glow

Swinging from
Star to star
Without getting

Enough of any
Looks Looks
So deepening

It's sure rain
Supply lumber
To feel number

At last
Silicon waves
Sand lengths

Silicon waves
Sand lengths
Stem to stern

Stem to stern
One-bite turnovers
Wave by

Wave by
One-bite turnovers
Hotter Hotter

Than suns
Times thousands
Stood hairs

Only a breeze
To some sense
Frozen tears

Licking clear
Epochal dalliance
Save beginning

Day dives up
Media muffins
Different Save

For occasions, whatnot
Gets set up
And housing starts

Down in the mouth
Hog sun
Fly rubs hands

Stay with it
Learn naught
After all

Learn naught
After all
Is said

Is said
Too well-done
Will you

Will you
Too well-done
Or won't you

Set stages
Doubtless
Owe payments on

Nervous system
Seen through
Not too blue

Language enters
Totally mezzanine
Ear off

Arms tightly around
Drop a beat
Fold left, as night

Beyond everybody
The whole tooth
Black out grandeur

So nice to be someplace
Familiar yet not familiar
Thought I saw a face

Hair all a mess
That's not true
Try again

That's not true
Try again
More bluer

More bluer
Great divide
Lie Multiply

Lie Multiply
Great divide
Honking lame buzzers

Pushing sideways
Memory hambone
Radiate soup

So, glow
Wised up feeders
Cleave gratefully

Brimming with ilk
Very very loose
But no closer

Crock of dawn
Opens wide
Without swallowing

Imagine your surprise
To find yourself
In the second person

Singalong singular
Seaview bungalow
Without moving

Even an inch
Gee, I don't
Know about that

Gee, I don't
Know about that
Sparkle and glow

Sparkle and glow
Moody airbrush edge
Let alone

Let alone
Moody airbrush edge
Shimmering divinish lands

You thought you heard
But maybe not
Maybe you hear again

Good food Good friends
Don't think so
Good time had by all

Slightly undone
According to
Later relating

Undated
Boy meets girlish
Type 100 WPM

Wash overhaul
Morning coffee
Mmm, good

Keep simple
And direct complications
With surety

Save something for
A rainy day
Blinds signal

A rainy day
Blinds signal
Not home

Not home
In the sense, away
Complete this picture

Complete this picture
In a sense, away
Looking up to

Down at
Across from
Donut perfection

Users leave
Bare taste of
Moving over

Slightly buttery
And commaless
But threading

Hovering around deals
Fans flutter hands
Adorning faces upturn

Impossible innocent
Mixes with bogus shit
The callout: gas station

Invented sweater-like
Blown out of proportion
Neverending the balloons

And never all at once
Fold vernal cues
Along green lines

Fold vernal cues
Along green lines
Hips bathe

Hips bathe
Quiet domestic fling
Wastebasket

Wastebasket
Quiet domestic fling
Big pain in the ass

Set back from view
Unnoticed details
Remain unnoticed

Except to secret
Barely concealed
Fleshly admirers

All link hands
In circling
The hard words

Tiptoe around
Stepping on your shit
Wouldn't you know

Mudroom heart
Coat each hook
With pants

Caught in liver beam
Fall across bare ass
Voice blends strings

You only thought
But didn't really
Think you had to

But didn't really
Think you had to
Recall

Recall
Anatomically correct
Inside out

Inside out
Anatomically correct
Along the lines

Last house
Before you're home
Weaving lungs

On point
Body memory
Just that

Thrown over shoulders
Imaginary wind
Realistic torrents

You may be
But I'm not
Where's that leave

Us unimaginable
Get away with
Goals we aim to please

Veer off
To parts unknown
Therefore

Hard to describe
Speak so beautiful
Heatseeking missile

Speak so beautiful
Heatseeking missile
Entrance

Entrance
Chimp grunt
Exit

Exit
Chimp grunt
Relaxed and invigorated

He had to've known
But he didn't
How couldn't he

It's easy
With all the powers
Of course

Pick a color
Any
Mean to you

Less than music
Ghostly sewing
Machine songs

Got to get going
Tree-to-tree moods
Swing from

Attention getting
Arm touches
Begin and end

Each sentence
Our song
Underdone

Our song
Underdone
Thumbs of love

Thumbs of love
Wish you
Well, were here

Well, were here
Wish you
Seem all right

Squawk Squish
Quiet evening
At home to who

Next 1/4 hour
Uplift upgrade
Sort of

Getting the idea
Little more
Left Left

How do you say
In universal language
Looking for

The next person
To talk to
Out of what

Sweat what
Care not in the world
Next to overdrive

Fifteen minutes
Either way
Sway in time to

Either way
Sway in time to
Switch back

Switch back
Snowshed irises
Lacquer day's ease

Lacquer day's ease
Snowshed irises
Make the grade

Willow search
For spring reasons
Echo things

Ear to ground
In principle
Slipper off

Dog chews through
And the next
Right of way

No strings
No past lives
Just you

And open road
Nothing between
No covers

Rub liberally
With extant love
Cinematic lotions

The real news
Make a person
To feel good

Make a person
To feel good
Right now!

Right now!
Paraparadise
Gotcha

Gotcha
Paraparadise
Notice more picture

Leave out
Any picture
Trip to vases

Thin with history
String dyed
To remember by

Bread
Butts
Coffee

As I stand
Or sit
Or lie down

On the mountain
The sea
Is great

Someplace else
Lapping at
Yapping coming

From yonder cloud
Oh, lively restaurant
Assemble me

Oh, lively restaurant
Assemble me
Gimme

Gimme
Food and drink
Quench thirst

Quench thirst
Food and drink
But first

And second
Maybe third
Yon rolling plains

Far as the eye
Can see
The ear

If I roll
Over off
No question

Have you lost
Your place
Or mind

Man or woman
Of the title
Wait up

Me but me
Open and shut
Joy pitstop

Dwindling anything
Don't knock
Walk right in

Don't knock
Walk right in
Deluge

Deluge
Shun all dops
Amino

Amino
Shun all dops
Quiet orphans

Invent a luggage
Smooth operator
Repeat clause

Battery power
High frequency
Sound nibbles

By rest
You mean
Not me

The strange
Part is
The strange

Part With
Always with
The moment

Of strangeness
Feeling out
Of it

But elastic
With frets
Live down

With frets
Live down
How strange

How strange
You feel
Follow up

Follow up
You feel
Stranger yet

But part
Elastic but
Sweat out

The triangle
Leads in
Often it

But as
Art ease
How translate

Something happens
Great
Nothing happens

Great
Whichever whatever
Twice nice

Agreeable mojo slipon
Root vegetable face
Sweetie

Ex out long for
Doggie on the skids
Talk too sun

Doggie on the skids
Talk too sun
Only one you

Only one you
Tide over
Another one

Another one
Tide over
Replacement touches

Orange drinks dunk
Under sudden squall
Whenever whichever

Record keepsakes
Rates said go
Gone

Wish lines answer
Hot
Quit shoving

Blue gulfs
Put on fur
Just a glimpse

Best is yet
What if
Don't come

What if
This tear
Douses

The end
Who'd notice
Not me

Who'd notice
Not me
You there?

You there?
About you
Care

Care
About you
Dwell awhile

Save the best
Way later
Insofar as

World root
Moist tenders
Imp drills

Speechless
Hairline crack
Hold that

Fuck happiness
Stop the mucous
Light's changing

In the back
So beautiful
Don't want to move

For fear
She'd be right
Get the wrong idea

Hiphugging
Swandive vocals
That's how life is

Swandive vocals
That's how life is
One day

One day
It's all
All over

All over
It's all
That's all

Get up
Change places
Leaving behind

So beautiful
Don't want to move
For fear

She'd be right
Get the wrong idea
Wrong

Don't forget
To put something in
A word for you

About great suffering
And other grand ideas
You pick up anywhere

The earth opens
And swallows you
To the core

Of your being
Too late
To do anything

Too late
To do anything
Stay

Stay
Your words be guides
Pray tell

Pray tell
Your words be guides
Verbs wash away bleeding

Orchestrate winds
With no strings
Adjective here

Days and nights
Do run on
Forget each sentence

The dog jumps
The cat runs
The train whistles

Time for dinner
Who wants to eat home
Bored shitless

Same old places
Same choices
Beyond boring

Someplace else
I've been there
Before Forget

The TV's on
Turn off the tube
Turn down easy does

Turn off the tube
Turn down easy does
It wanders

It wanders
Food for thought
Somehow redeem

Somehow redeem
Food for thought
So ordered

Can you bleeve
Thunk wikowover
Lamp swift

Frid morv lab
Big sullen quit
But ak soup

And theoretically
Lit whiff
Pick ripe

By empty
I mean empties
Pick hit

Same people
Get on
Get off Get off

Can't imagine
Where they go
What they do

Each day, there
I'd be fevered
If I wasn't flavored

I'd be fevered
If I wasn't flavored
Cloudy effort

Cloudy effort
Lead gaze skyward
Press forward

Press forward
Lead gaze skyward
Where are

Shoot, sunblind
Shade slips on
Over dress

That man
Is standing
In the middle

Of the street
Watching a coat
On the ground

Your driver
Left a little
Bit late

And will
Get to you
A little bit

Late Please
Excuse
The delay

I have no driver
The golf ball
Has

The golf ball
Has
A driver

A driver
Staring directly
At it

At it
Staring directly
Ready to

Tee off
Which means
To make angry

I'm not angry
I'm pleasant
Maybe

The baby driver
Is pleasant
A little delay

The notes are interesting
There are things to learn
From and about

About six inches
From your ear
The words stop

Birdlike in descent
Can you call it back
The mind is wandering

Look for a place
To light
It's getting dark

To light
It's getting dark
No need

No need
To understand
What's in mind

What's in mind
To understand
Get inside

The body
Make each step count
As you step outside

Stretching each muscle
Attaching each muscle
To bone up on

Believe the person before
Returning to the text
And parabolic faxes

It was
As if
I took

A few
Weeks off
To attend

My own death
Gives me
A look

Froze me
In my tracks
You follow

In my tracks
You follow
Letter

Letter
To better
Grip on

Grip on
To better
Liken

Please digress
Please undress
Please leave

Trees alone
Dot eyes
With leases

Open to
Renewal
Renegotiate

Walk over
And out of
The moviola

The word for
I've been searching
Brain rack

How you say
Tangy dreams
Leave lips

Drawn inward
Exaggerate shoulder
Lay me down

Exaggerate shoulder
Lay me down
Take stairs

Take stairs
Two at a time
Call morning

Call morning
Two at a time
No exaggeration

Each morning
Imagine
What to do

And who with
Will I wake
Follow up

In the wakeup
Earthbound thirst
Vine coolers

Asked questions
Barely concentrate
Bluff ah well

Self offered up
Totally jumps groove
Vocal takes

Local customs
Fascinating study
In starving

Seething snatches
Record the minutes
Brief meeting

Record the minutes
Brief meeting
Read letter into

Read letter into
Fiddle moves
Bow deeply

Bow deeply
Fiddle moves
Manage smile

The one you last
For eternity
Saw me with

In half pisses off
Forever
All hope fades

Explanation
To follow
Please excuse

Once familiar road
Miss the line
Your thing do

American retail hump
Erects speed bumps
Slow tourists down

Pictures snap away
Literally eye-catching
Discuss each iris

So and so, you bet
Spiffy items program
Digression again

Spiffy items program
Digression again
Vaguely orifice

Vaguely orifice
Heartbreaking bottle
A little too familiar

A little too familiar
Heartbreaking bottle
Casual mention

Eternal black
False front building
Construe a town

Cue ponds suggest
This would be great
Maybe another blue

More orangy
Putting people out
Behind the scenes

Touch my food
With your tongue
Doesn't wake up

Your terrible sleep
Dissolve in rapture
Twist with rumors

Embroider validation
With a contents
Worthy of a jacket

Color-coded jewel
Wistful deep look
Frag smoky earth

Wistful deep look
Frag smoky earth
Blue frame ring

Blue frame ring
Relief shouts along
Moonglow shoots

Moonglow shoots
Relief shouts along
Torn off wrung out

Appealing, and now
Can hear it
Dump Dump

Mango figure out
Allege curve
Remove from yourself

Cross at right smile
Album cover instead
Out one chair

Important to who
Like, any good
Sweaty Different

Flat against
Old doors
To the future

Butterfly-minded
No reason to
Lie around

Humid and mopey
Give a look
But act cool

Give a look
But act cool
Someday tell

Someday tell
Picture was like
No mouth

No mouth
Picture was like
As not

To mean something
Remember
You come from

There Remember
Watch
Where you go

Weather as here
Will do
As gun

Like my shoes
Don't they look
Nice Nice

Cavalcade of heels
Brushes each ganglion
With butter

I hear
Then I don't hear
A couple months

I worry
Sitting around
On my mind

Sitting around
On my mind
Oh, clerk

Oh, clerk
Maybe it's me
Beyond this and that

Beyond this and that
Maybe it's me
Do what you have to

Make a go of oh
Trail leads away
Frizzle crownish heart

Cold call highlights
Call waiting
DOOM

Birds rap the view
It looked like
Embroidering need

Said (with grin)
For lunch
Hand saying, suggest

Guest list incidentals
Frown the keys
Thinking over Staying

Over feel just right
Dropping in coatless
Participle hip

Rave notices
Notice the curve
Lattice climb aboard

Notice the curve
Lattice climb aboard
Fix kiss

Fix kiss
Inner room undertow
Control console

Control console
Inner room undertow
Foot saying, all best

Out of the way
Ceiling worship tumbles
Through clothes

Marking inflection
For pointing out
Smile buried in stone

Stapled nerves
Cut to night's argument
Hasped with luck

Running totals
Hold off dawn
Without Quik Pik

Scabby whoopdedoo
Cut costs and lays off
Beauty's carry forwards

Dazzle with needless suffering
No fools no fast talkers
No festive enchantment

Heatseeking and unassuming
Twinbill bird calls
Advise travel card views

Twinbill bird calls
Advise travel card views
Feeling quarantine

Feeling quarantine
Out of guarantees
Swallow soundscape

Swallow soundscape
Out of guarantees
Pull over to right

Tie one tie on
Clipon sunray bone
Upgrade deluge

Needle pastels
Crank with despair
Let's see what happens

Traffic reeks open mind
Reflecting public spins
Wages reflect wrong wins

Other films
Drain fresh vinyl
Through a straw

Dim light hair fuss
Reaches into bag
Funny thing

Which means staring
At 4 walls
The whole idea

Gasping each nuance
I'm not crying
Entering the funnel

I'm not crying
Entering the funnel
From what

From what
You said enough
Remember thinking

Remember thinking
You said enough
Gone fading aisles

But why
Feel like telling
Lots of flame

Flashed look
Gulp down with
Thirsty worry

Believe me
Even closer
Jet takes off

About right
Sleep over
The hard parts

Stuff
You don't
Want to know

About About
Right in front
Your nose

Your everything
Take down
Put down

Take down
Put down
Forever

Forever
Close the book
Kiss

Kiss
Close the book
Backsie frontsie

Know at once
Cloud over
Pro Am

Shakes platform
Who needs
A permit

To breathe
Momentarily
Handy calendar

I said
That I would
Getting ready

First thing ask
Everybody agrees
Insect flesh

Decide aspects
Duds everywhere
You up

Pay to do
Our children
Have to know

Our children
Have to know
That

That
Win nightmare
Outright

Outright
Win nightmare
Change

In back
Like eternity
Is another

Stupid excuse
For some shit
Slap together

Palm off on
First second
Seen

Another sugar?
Wingnut purity
Around attitude

Around enough
Look out for
Don't call me

Call the other plum
In line with
Edge skates

Willingly or otherwise
Talk serious
Tell all

Talk serious
Tell all
Less fair

Less fair
Between outpourings
Flip

Flip
Between outpourings
Flop down

Day fall blue plate
Wake up next to
Be more generous

Didn't think
It would me
Anything

Goes with
Tonight's topic
Coffee clouds you

Where were we
Getting out of here
Getting away

That's easy
Simple planet noise
Graced with freshets

One long coffee
Too short
Laced with dice

Die happy
Wipe that grin
Off shiteating

Wipe that grin
Off shiteating
Missing something

Missing something
Today's special
Kindred spirit

Kindred spirit
Today's special
Climb off watch

Wheezing head
Smoking furiously
Pure manifestos

Doors can use
Voices as oils
Tongue piano hinge

When you make
Your selection
Known Paw

Something tells me
Some little bird
Too late

Big lawn sun
Is setting us up
For aerobic balustrades

Looped with beltways
Astonished into pants
And folksong long division

Aftermath slices
Takeout after all
Carrying charges

Take out after all
Carrying charges
Set to blow

Set to blow
Windows of opportunity
Subvocal pines

Subvocal pines
Windows of opportunity
Blabbing free foam

Elevated by tide
To certain aluminum
Toggled with wishes

Believing myself
To be ready
To wear thin

I could be
Fooling myself
Smack forehead

Smoking
Like a fish
Come upstairs

Two at a time
Not people
The fish

Season changes clue
Mentally
More salt less pep

Shaving next morning
Inch Square Per
Lowball no cal

Inch Square Per
Lowball no cal
Lives enter left

Lives enter left
Glue dry
Fire brimstone gym

Fire brimstone gym
Glue dry
Offhand headlines

Aqua lunges
I gather
This is the ceiling

These aren't
Whatever you hear
Words set

In stone
Amazing toxins
Clear on point

With reference
To perimeter
Where edge is

Some character's bridge
Float in a glass
House on fire

With fire as a subject
Too personal
Instinct draws away

Unseen parallel
Give any devil due
Do the deal

Give any devil due
Do the deal
Mint morning highlights

Mint morning highlights
Lowlife pardon me
Exact change

Exact change
Lowlife pardon me
Take a number

Earn in amber
Sleep's shadow
Starting shallow end

Admire how awful
Add admiration to
Birdlike dermatology

Tracks in sand
Tide out
Glad wrapped

Home
An hour ago
Change clothes

Dinner
Drink
Half drunk

Read paper
Any
Day begun

At low
Point to
How come

Point to
How come
Who cares

Who cares
Become some
Otherwise

Otherwise
Become some
Local moe

Dig holes
They come in
Frappes

Because
Loose lips
Link hips

Sleepers
Slip in
Keepers

Cut to
Quick brown fox
Out there

When I could
Breathe
Could it be

Magic Tape
Rolling hills
Good night's rest

Doing a thing
Stranger light
Radiates friends

Stranger light
Radiates friends
Be grammar

Be grammar
Yonder nervous cow
Mid riff

Mid riff
Yonder nervous cow
So...I was

Thinking past
Glam minutes
Under vitamins

Phase in
Equally slowly
With platinum

Point to prove
Puppy latte
Nail clues

4:37 PM
Urge to call
Someone in

California
Who I know
There Will

They feed me
When I get
Off, food

And lodging
Go through
My book

Go through
My book
Talked recently

Talked recently
Ask after
Deep down

Deep down
Ask after
Those, don't

Usually talk
With What's
The comma

Doing
Three time
Zones earlier

Subject to
Who cares
Approved

Not enough
To do
Becomes too

Much to
Do What
About now

Easy listening
Air glide
Bottle neck

Human strings
Pull out of
Dive

Pull out of
Dive
Libretto

Libretto
Fasteners
Without notes

Without notes
Fasteners
Live once

In awhile
Alba dosed
Won short

How about
Food Food
Reading matter

Leaves off
The reason
Thought

Itsy pleasure centers
Feel free to leave
Well enough alone

Summoning forth
Bad spells
Tender spoons

How do you spell
Fork Which road
Supplies a take on

Heart eaten out
On public transport
Wheels turn

On public transport
Wheels turn
Crack smoke

Crack smoke
Believe me
Track soak

Track soak
Believe me
She always never

Comes
Your welcome
Home

All hair
All the time
Stop Dime

Uptown and
And very
Way down

Find myself
Lost and found
Like a glove

Fitting
Crawling into
Your universe

Creeping
You out
On all fours

Alive at five
And that's
You recall

And that's
You recall
The news

The news
Within the muse
Led on

Led on
Within the muse
Finger by finger

As if inkling
Calligraphy sunset
Buttons hither

Refreshment stands
For salvation
Each bottle redeems

For we are
Plenty wandering
Torn wonder

Am so inclined
Lean into
For thought of

Leading indicators
Prize research
Go 4 2

Rain and wind
Whoop it up
In car alarms

Be party to
Nothing means
No you

Nothing means
No you
How do

How do
Back into
Over and under

Over and under
Back into
Bulletin

Booked up
And don't look
Now

Any other dawn
Otherwise
Down upon

A person
Needs a rest
From that person

Dog gone
But where
But who

Nasty oldster
Reign supreme
No shine

Pressure built
Pressure mounted
No stress

Syllabic lust
Didn't they
Use to

Didn't they
Use to
And one day

And one day
They die
Sniff

Sniff
They die
Unleash

Light up
Working
On timelessness

Eyes go with
In suit
No divider

Double lines
Make sure
You know

Sometime
New right
Tomorrow is

Never always
No matter
How personal

Wearing a footstole
I see
I run into

Another day
Where is
Were you

Where is
Were you
Fear for

Fear for
Hippo theory
Lump with

Lump with
Hippo theory
Home tool

Don't let
Anything bother
You better

And without
Chemical lounges
Decline interview

These are
My people
A known fact

Eggs
Break
Dawn

On
Walk
Out

Complete
With
Muff

Fuses
Pipe
In

Pipe
In
Back

Back
It
Up

Up
It
To

Where
Forget
About

It
Gets
Better

Get
Up
Soon

The next day
Is tomorrow
More or less

All tied up
Can't take it
Keep trying

Something is
Messing
Keep trying

But each time
Physically
All told

Physically
All told
Speedy

Speedy
Feature steps
Minor memoir

Minor memoir
Feature steps
No matter

How hard
You think
You wish

Ah So
This is
Some food

Ah Maybe
So long
Come again

What
You don't
Seem to

Realize I'm
Crazy out
Whatever

You, whoever
Feel free
To leave

The tree
Freefall
Believe me

Freefall
Believe me
Who you gonna

Who you gonna
Run to
When well

When well
Run to
But over

So what
You do
The future

Think how
Often when
Take place

When
You do
What do

Driver
With one hand
Talking away

A mile
A minute
Away

Then some
Start lead
Varying plum

Turn coins
Corner moans
Ass swivels

Corner moans
Ass swivels
Fishing for

Fishing for
U bang G
Wheat frobes

Wheat frobes
U bang G
But let

Small wonder
This book
Thy laboratory

For is writ
For witness
Then some

So shall you
Pass for
Saving grace

Push has come
To shove
No snap

I'll write
It down
Too lay back

Policy requires
You keep in place
Your face

Between mums
Shove pushes
Close shave

Shove pushes
Close shave
Upon paths

Upon paths
Open gems
Frill style

Frill style
Open gems
Open wider

This friendly fire
To have
Is not

The first thing
On out
My mind

Sweet potato
Live far
Golden calf

Snowed under
Skels talk
Under themselves

No rings phone
No piqued boos
No wandering eye

Dark clouds roll
Belong to thee
Slightly overheard

Unanswered bell
Cup crumple
Swingle bible law

Cup crumple
Swingle bible law
Too pup

Too pup
To heat your dog
Chow down

Chow down
To heat your dog
Hickory armpits

Liquid smoke
Ekes out
Desire remnants

Torn to recognize
Underline
Shady ewer

Annoint forever
Pass the shade
Seamless shadows

When I look
Around I see
Red

Tonight's color
Of wishful thinking
Made bonnet

Succeed where
Others have wailed
Come what pay

Calls cease
Don't hear anymore
These problems

Don't hear anymore
These problems
Mystery deepens

Mystery deepens
But for what
Wafer thin

Wafer thin
But for what
Safety moon

Everything takes place
Despise your mats
Waistline coda

Good thing
Home early
Allure looks

Can you believe
You actually
Stay off put

So rare
To get
A really good

Hamburger
When you start
From what you

Consider nothing
Nothing stops you
Except U

Turn off at
The service station
Lights greet you

The service station
Lights greet you
Night's young

Night's young
Only you
With NG

With NG
Only you
Remembers

To forget
You forget
Brought you

Here
First place
I don't know

Catch up
Dunno
More U

Big thought
Big moment
Amongst friends

Share food
Try this
Mmmm

Aimless milestones
Establish cornices
Things to don't

But not mind
Clear pass
Pass through

Clear pass
Pass through
Phrase hooks

Phrase hooks
Sullen pharoahs
Coal binds

Coal binds
Sullen pharoahs
Cite ancestors

To the city
Layer complaints
As showers

Clouds move in
But fair
Putter arrange

Free to have
Your opinion
Minus ion

And then I realized
That was me
In the past tense

Answering the phone
Worrying
Thinking about

The comma
Why bother
Lots of play

Fuck calling
Sad leaving
How often

Sad leaving
How often
Comes up

Comes up
Same thought
Something like

Something like
Same thought
But unique

Which is when
Mist web
Bound to fail

As can and won't
Work
Off and toward

This is now
Designated so
Not here

I'm trying
To enjoy this
Do something

About the brakes
Take in a movie
Little smile, maybe

This is America
And
What the fuck

Which brings in
Hamburger
Chicken

Hamburger
Chicken
What that's about

What that's about
Next to last
This is it

This is it
Next to last
Kind of shit

Summing up
What comes up
Which is a cup

Let me know
This is too much
Combine with

Too little
But awful small
Recedes into

114

Airbrush hammer
Crystal infantries
I not me

In another development
From when
True love

Free ozone
Makes for
An afternoon

Curving gradually
Besides the baby
Who loves you

Besides the baby
Who loves you
Cannot fail

Cannot fail
To give notice
Perpetual twinning

Perpetual twinning
To give notice
Its due

Chrome to
That special blue
You owe

It to yourself
To glue
To wear

Glad to hear
Hope well
All best

Came in
Along with
Tempt to

Fans don't count
Except all hands
Attend takers

Too dressed
Stop by
Depend on

Full morning
Run into
Relax at home

Run into
Relax at home
You recognize

You recognize
Lit folks
Alongside frays

Alongside frays
Lit folks
Send them on

Send them on
To arrive
At a verb

To so
Feels grave
Fits like

Unfold leaf
Rakes vowels
As primes

ROOF BOOKS

- Andrews, Bruce. **EX WHY ZEE.** 112p. $10.95.
- Andrews, Bruce. **Getting Ready To Have Been Frightened**. 116p. $7.50.
- Benson, Steve. **Blue Book**. Copub. with The Figures. 250p. $12.50
- Bernstein, Charles. **Islets/Irritations**. 112p. $9.95.
- Bernstein, Charles (editor). **The Politics of Poetic Form**. 246p. $12.95; cloth $21.95.
- Brossard, Nicole. **Picture Theory**. 188p. $11.95.
- Child, Abigail. **Scatter Matrix**. 79p. $9.95.
- Davies, Alan. **Active 24 Hours**. 100p. $5.
- Davies, Alan. **Signage**. 184p. $11.
- Davies, Alan. **Rave**. 64p. $7.95.
- Day, Jean. **A Young Recruit**. 58p. $6.
- Di Palma, Ray. **Motion of the Cypher**. 112p. $10.95.
- Di Palma, Ray. **Raik**. 100p. $9.95.
- Doris, Stacy. **Kildare**. 104p. $9.95.
- Dreyer, Lynne. **The White Museum**. 80p. $6.
- Edwards, Ken. **Good Science**. 80p. $9.95.
- Eigner, Larry. **Areas Lights Heights**. 182p. $12, $22 (cloth).
- Gizzi, Michael. **Continental Harmonies**. 92p. $8.95.
- Gottlieb, Michael. **Ninety-Six Tears**. 88p. $5.
- Grenier, Robert. **A Day at the Beach**. 80p. $6.
- Grosman, Ernesto. **The XUL Reader: An Anthology of Argentine Poetry (1981–1996)**. 167p. $14.95.
- Hills, Henry. **Making Money**. 72p. $7.50. VHS videotape $24.95. Book & tape $29.95.
- Huang Yunte. **SHI: A Radical Reading of Chinese Poetry.** 76p. $9.95
- Hunt, Erica. **Local History**. 80 p. $9.95.
- Inman, P. **Criss Cross**. 64 p. $7.95.
- Inman, P. **Red Shift**. 64p. $6.
- Lazer, Hank. **Doublespace**. 192 p. $12.
- Mac Low, Jackson. **Representative Works: 1938–1985**. 360p. $12.95, $18.95 (cloth).
- Mac Low, Jackson. **Twenties**. 112p. $8.95.
- Moriarty, Laura. **Rondeaux**. 107p. $8.
- Neilson, Melanie. **Civil Noir**. 96p. $8.95.
- Pearson, Ted. **Planetary Gear**. 72p. $8.95.
- Perelman, Bob. **Virtual Reality**. 80p. $9.95.
- Perelman, Bob. **The Future of Memory.** 120p. $14.95.
- Piombino, Nick, **The Boundary of Blur**. 128p. $13.95.
- Raworth, Tom. **Clean & Will-Lit**. 106p. $10.95.
- Robinson, Kit. **Balance Sheet**. 112p. $11.95.

- ❏ Robinson, Kit. **Democracy Boulevard.** 104p. $9.95.
- ❏ Robinson, Kit. **Ice Cubes**. 96p. $6.
- ❏ Scalapino, Leslie. **Objects in the Terrifying Tense Longing from Taking Place.** 88p. $9.95.
- ❏ Seaton, Peter. **The Son Master**. 64p. $5.
- ❏ Sherry, James. **Popular Fiction**. 84p. $6.
- ❏ Silliman, Ron. **The New Sentence**. 200p. $10.
- ❏ Silliman, Ron. **N/O**. 112p. $10.95.
- ❏ Stephans, Brian Kim. **Free Space Comix**.
- ❏ Templeton, Fiona. **Cells of Release**. 128p. with photographs. $13.95.
- ❏ Templeton, Fiona. **YOU—The City**. 150p. $11.95.
- ❏ Ward, Diane. **Human Ceiling**. 80p. $8.95.
- ❏ Ward, Diane. **Relation**. 64p. $7.50.
- ❏ Watten, Barrett. **Progress**. 122p. $7.50.
- ❏ Weiner, Hannah. **We Speak Silent**. 76 p. $9.95
- ❏ Yasusada, Araki. **Doubled Flowering: From the Notebooks of Araki Yasusada.** 272p. $14.95.

Mark the boxes of the books you wish to order and send a check to:
Segue Foundation, 303 East 8th Street, New York, NY 10009